LIVING VALUES

STATEMENTS

Excerpted from Section One of the book,
Living Values: A Guidebook,
a Publication in Honor of the
Fiftieth Anniversary of the United Nations

LIVING VALUES STATEMENTS

First Edition November 1995

ISBN 1-886872-01-5

Published by the Brahma Kumaris World Spiritual University,
Literature Department, 65 Pound Lane, London NW10 2HH UK

There are Brahma Kumaris Centres in over 62 countries worldwide.

© Copyright 1995 Brahma Kumaris World Spiritual University
65 Pound Lane, London NW10 2HH UK

Printed by Waterside Litho, Chesham, UK

Available in other languages

CONTENTS

PREFACE

Dadi Janki,
Co-Administrative Head,
Brahma Kumaris World Spiritual University,
Mt. Abu, India

At a time of crisis, we are again at a point of recognizing the need for values. An orphaned child feels insecure, unloved, and unwanted; one without a life of values feels the same. Values are our "parents" - the human soul is nurtured by the values it holds. A sense of security and comfort comes through values in one's life.

Values are the treasure of life, making humans wealthy and rich. Values are friends, bringing happiness in life. A life filled with values is a life of self-respect and dignity. The soul is able to come closer to God, and life becomes real and meaningful. Values bring independence and freedom, expand the capacity to be self-sufficient, and liberate one from external influences. The soul develops the ability to discern truth and to follow the path of truth.

Values offer protection, and one who experiences this is able to share this protection with others. Values bring empowerment, and it becomes possible to remove weaknesses and defects. As the innate goodness of the individual is concentrated on values, the link with God becomes strong and clear. Service is then rendered to others through thoughts, words, and actions. A soul with values is not trapped by any limited desires or attractions, but remains stable in the unlimited.

Values open the heart and transform human nature so that life is filled with compassion and humility.

As we develop values within the self, we share the fragrance of those values with the world around us, and in this way move forward to a better world.

INTRODUCTION

The Value Statements in this booklet uphold principles and philosophy which address the universal aspect of spiritual and moral values as a basis for living one's life. Discussing each value in both conceptual and practical terms, the statements are designed to encourage the reader to think about, reflect on, understand, realize, assimilate, and practice 12 core values: Cooperation, Freedom, Happiness, Honesty, Humility, Love, Peace, Respect, Responsibility, Simplicity, Tolerance, and Unity. Since values are interconnected, to recognize and explore the significance of one value is to experience the unlimited treasure store of underlying and supporting values.

The statements are deep. Reflecting on one point, sentence, or paragraph – and realizing and absorbing its significance – takes time and thought. In that process, the reader can journey inside as deeply and honestly as he or she wishes, using each value as a guide to discover what lies within the self. That effort promises a more meaningful definition of one's higher purpose in life. The individual can uncover a capacity to stretch beyond the limits of current reality and recognize his or her full potential, not only in relation to the self but also to the wider world.

In choosing or becoming aware of values we adopt as the motivations for our behavior, we assign worth or importance to an aspect of life, which, in turn, influences how we approach life. Today the majority of people are largely influenced and define their true worth by material values such as social position, monetary worth, external appearance, or personal possessions. That misrepresentation of the source of true worth creates cultures of accumulation, possessiveness, selfishness, and greed and is the root cause of conflict, exploitation, poverty, and tension in the world. True worth comes from realizing the dignity and value of the individual and of the sacredness or divine nature of human life. A person who really understands his or her own inherent worth and respects that of others will come to know that worth is not something assigned by external factors, but rather, comes from a source that is universal and eternal.

There is universal recognition of a hierarchy of values which ascends from the lower material values to those higher spiritual values such as peace, love, care, selflessness, and generosity. Such higher order values transcend the uniqueness of humanity's richly diverse cultural, philosophical, and social heritage, forming a common bedrock on which to build not only friendly international relations but also mutual benefit in one-on-one interactions.

The 12 higher values described are core values fundamental to the well being of humanity as a whole. They will touch the core of the individual, perhaps inspiring positive change, which can contribute to world transformation. The world will automatically become a better place when each individual becomes a better person.

*C*OOPERATION

One who cooperates receives
cooperation.

The method to give
cooperation is to use the energy of the
mind to create vibrations of good wishes
and pure feelings for the others and for
the task.

By remaining detached, objective, and
influenced by innermost values and not
external circumstances, subtle cooperation
in the form of wisdom emerges.

Human achievement is like a mountain range with cliffs, crags, slopes, and valleys. To aim for excellence in collective achievement is to aspire to climb to the crowning point. The endeavor requires each climber to be equipped with essential skills and knowledge and good amounts of determination and will power. However, no climb should ever be undertaken without the most indispensable piece of equipment: the safety rope of cooperation. Cooperation ensures equanimity, empowerment, easiness, and enthusiasm. Cooperation provides the means for each climber to take a step, no matter how small, and for those steps collectively to reach the pinnacle.

Mutual Benefit

Cooperation is not a bargaining game in which one person's success is achieved at the expense or exclusion of the success of others. The constant aim of cooperation is mutual benefit in human interactions; it is governed by the principle of mutual respect. Courage, consideration, caring, and sharing provide a foundation from which cooperation as a process can be developed.

If the power of discrimination is sharp at the time a person, group, or nation needs cooperation and the accurate method is applied, there will be success in human interactions and relations. The method can be as simple as providing an explanation, giving love or support, or listening. However, if there is lack of power to discern the type of cooperation needed and the correct method to give that, success in the form of agreement and contentment will not be experienced. That can be likened to a doctor not accurately diagnosing the illness. Instead of getting well, the patient would experience complications created by the treatment.

Cooperation is possible when there is easiness, not heaviness. Easiness means being sincere and generous of spirit. Such liberality makes one worthy of receiving cooperation from everyone. If one has faith and confidence in others, that, in turn, builds faith and confidence in others. Such feelings produce a comfortable environment of empowerment, respect, support, and togetherness.

Everyone's Responsibility

Cooperation is everyone's responsibility, yet it takes courage and inner strength to facilitate the process. Sometimes those who take on the responsibility become the target for insult and criticism. Fundamental preparations are required to create an internal support mechanism through which such individuals are able to protect themselves and maintain equanimity and poise. The necessary attitude is one of detachment, in which nothing is taken personally. By remaining detached, objective, and influenced by innermost values and not external circumstances, subtle cooperation in the form of wisdom emerges. To look at another with an attitude of love and cooperation - even after having been "defamed" by that person - is known as having merciful vision. The outlook is infused with understanding, forgiveness, tolerance, patience, and empathy. One with such a nature more easily facilitates the removal of any "grid-locks of non-cooperation" which may have been stalling progress.

Cooperation requires recognizing the unique role of every individual while maintaining a sincere and positive attitude. Positive thoughts within the self automatically and easily create the feeling of cooperation within the minds of others. The method to give cooperation is to use the energy of the mind to create vibrations of good wishes and pure feelings for the others and for the task. That affects the atmosphere in a positive and subtle way. The collective vibrations of such pure and subtle effort prepare the ground for open and profound deliberations and a successful round of cooperation.

Time Is Now

Cooperation with time and with the natural order of events brings patience. Time is valuable because it always offers unique opportunities to achieve what is best and what is necessary at the moment it is meant to be. Time cooperates with each person if one chooses to recognize its importance.

In the process of world transformation, the time is now for each person to lend a finger of cooperation - if not with mind, then with body; if not with body, then with wealth; if not with wealth, then with encouraging or urging others to cooperate. If each were to lend one small finger, together the mountain would be lifted! And when the subtle ties which join us together in universal brotherhood are recognized as unbreakable, then cooperation will become inevitable, and together we will reach new and greater heights!

$\mathscr{F}$REEDOM

*Full freedom functions only when
rights are balanced with responsibilities
and choice is balanced with conscience.*

*The most potent power to put an end
to internal and external wars is
the human conscience.*

Freedom is a precious gift which promises an experience of liberation and a feeling of no limits - as if the earth, the skies, and the seas are at one's service!

The concepts of freedom and liberty have fascinated human beings. One of the greatest aspirations in the world today is to be free. People want the freedom to lead a life of purpose, to select freely a lifestyle in which they and their children can grow healthily and can flourish through the work of their hands, heads, and hearts. They want to do and go as they please and to enjoy social, political, and economic rights and privileges. In short, they want the freedom to choose, to risk, and to succeed!

True Freedom

Freedom can be understood mistakenly to be a vast and unlimited umbrella which gives permission to "do what I like, when I like, to whomever I like." That concept is misleading and a misuse of choice. True freedom is exercised and experienced when parameters are defined and understood. Parameters are determined by the principle that everyone has equally the same rights. For example, the rights to peace, happiness, and justice - regardless of religion, culture, or gender - are innate. To violate the rights of one or more in order to free the self, family, or nation is a misuse of freedom. That kind of misuse usually backfires, eventually imposing a condition of constraint, and in some cases, oppression - for the violated and the violator. Misuse creates conflict and imbalance - in the self, in others, and in nature - and the result of that is evident in the modern world.

Full freedom functions only when rights are balanced with responsibilities and choice is balanced with conscience. There cannot be the experience of freedom, individually or collectively, if attention and effort are focused only on rights and choice. When rights and choice are misunderstood or misused, debts are incurred - mentally, physically, spiritually, socially, economically, politically, and so on.

Safeguarding Freedom

To safeguard freedom, individuals must not excuse, as an example, the following sentiment and the actions resulting from it: "A little greed, a little aggression, a little anger is necessary to keep people or things in their place." Such a compromise, beginning as a trace of violation, quickly multiplies; other wrong sentiments and actions are then justified. Harmful or negative thoughts, words, or actions produce equal reactions, as do beneficial and positive sentiments and actions. In other words, what is sown is reaped. That is the natural law of action known as the Law of Karma. It means that, individually or collectively, positively or negatively, accounts will be settled and debts incurred will be paid.

One of the key functions of a government, an institution, or any system which has taken the responsibility to serve is to safeguard, promote, and guarantee freedom at three levels: 1) within the individual, which includes a wide range of physical and mental dimensions from preventing torture, pain, or suffering to encouraging self-actualization and self-expression; 2) within groups, societies, or countries, which is demonstrated through justice and equality in assuring human rights; and 3) within nature, which means total respect for natural laws, which are constant and unshakable and which ensure nature's right to an unpolluted life.

Freedom From Bondage

As trustees of the precious gift of freedom and in reaction to violations of freedom, we continue to sense the imperative to liberate peoples and states from the "iron chains of oppression." Yet, even with independence, individuals remain bound to their own "iron chains" of lust, anger, attachment, ego, greed, and violence. They continue to "do battle" internally, within their own minds, and it is from that "battlefield" that all wars are born.

Thus, there needs to be freedom from complications and confusion within the mind, intellect, and heart of human beings. Such battles may be experienced in the forms of wasteful or negative thinking influenced by the "iron chains." Even if one were to conquer gross anger, there may continue to be subtle feelings of hostility, revenge, or ill will which must be examined, understood, and let go. Each one's nature is unique. However, to adopt easiness, lightness, and mercy in consciousness, attitude, and outlook is proactive - and the means to be free from the influence of negative personality traits.

Ultimate freedom is liberation from bondages created from acting in the consciousness of the body - out of attachments to the self and its senses; to others; and to worldly possessions. Liberation is releasing oneself from such attachments. That does not suggest one would not be loved and loving. On the contrary, having become more independent within, one's outside demeanor would reflect a less dependent and more loving nature.

Self-transformation begins the process of world transformation. The world will not be free from war and injustice until individuals themselves are set free. The most potent power to put an end to internal and external wars - and to set souls free - is the human conscience. Any act of freedom, when aligned with the human conscience, is liberating, empowering, and ennobling.

HAPPINESS

Through the power of truth
there is wealth, and through the power of
peace there is health.

Together they give happiness.

Happiness is earned by those whose
actions, attitude, and attributes are
pure and selfless.

Paradise, Heaven, Aquarius, El Dorado, the Garden of Eden, the Garden of Allah, Utopia, Vaikunth, the Fields of Osiris, and the Golden Age are names by which a world of peace, purity, and prosperity has been remembered. In such a place, each human being is like a flower, a country like a bouquet of flowers, and the world like a garden of flowers. The sun, the sustainer, shines upon the garden with golden rays, flooding it with newness and nobility. The Gate of Happiness stands open, welcoming the human family to the Golden Garden. In the past, the world was such a garden. It will become that again. Simply to have that faith is cause for celebration.

Pursuit of Happiness

At present, many question the purpose of life. Some are tired of living, others have lost hope. Some make effort to earn wealth, believing that will bring happiness. Some who have wealth may not have health, and that causes unhappiness. Some choose certain professions, believing that will give happiness. Others seek happiness through relationships. Yet, however much happiness such measures may bring, they are temporary and limited sources of the material world, and in many instances, they bring equal amounts of sorrow and unhappiness.

Such inability to hold onto pure and lasting happiness results from bankruptcy of spiritual values and powers. Awareness and application of spiritual truths provide the true source of happiness. Through the power of truth there is wealth, and through the power of peace there is health. Together they give happiness. Like a tonic, spiritual knowledge makes the hopeless ones hopeful. Pure happiness returns to anyone who seeks such new and hopeful horizons. Important things forgotten are remembered. The feeling can be compared to returning home – as you see the trees and smell the breeze, you know you are nearing something close to your heart!

The warmth and comfort of happiness is hidden within the self. When individuals turn within and take strength from the internal powers of peace and silence, they revive their virtues and allow the mercury of happiness to rise. The soul becomes open to the secrets of how to live in an interdependent way without becoming a victim of the material world which by its very nature robs people of their happiness. The vault of spiritual knowledge holds treasures on how to live and act with truth. True actions are pure, and purity is the mother of happiness and comfort. True actions bring strength and happiness to the self and pleasure to others. Spiritual treasures include guidelines on how to reform character and activity. For many, self-progress and personal transformation are keys that unlock the Gate of Happiness.

Happiness of Mind

People speak of peace of mind. Happiness of mind is a state of peace in which there is no upheaval or violence. Peace within the self creates faith in the intellect. The flute of happiness plays softly and constantly in the minds of those who have such faith. No matter how adverse or challenging a situation may be, there is fearlessness, for the power of faith gives the guarantee of ultimate victory. As the intellect becomes enlightened by spiritual wisdom, there are less mood swings and doubts in the heart. An individual becomes better able to pay off debts of pain and sorrow while maintaining a healthy account of happiness. In a world where all relationships have accounts of happiness and sorrow, the greatest lesson to be learned about being happy is: "Give happiness and take happiness, don't give sorrow and take sorrow."

Happiness is prosperity which comes from self-sovereignty. Self-sovereignty means being master over the mind, intellect, personality traits, and physical senses of the body; being complete with all powers and virtues; and attaining a perfect balance between masculine and feminine characteristics. There is that state of perfection within each human soul. On the spiritual quest in search of such perfection, the intellect goes through a process of discovering its divine nature.

Unlimited Fortune

Happiness does not carry a price tag. It cannot be bought, sold, or bargained for. Happiness is earned by those whose actions, attitude, and attributes are pure and selfless. In other words, the quality of the consciousness and activities of individuals determines the richness of life.

However, social, economic, and political stability are cited as sources of happiness and enjoyment in life. Yet, whenever any one of those areas is in disarray, the mercury of happiness in people drops. When all resources are focused on socioeconomic infrastructure at the expense of the development of the spiritual and moral character of the people, then priorities in life are misrepresented and there is a gradual erosion of happiness. Moral and spiritual values help reassess priorities and allow for proactive and preventive measures to take place at opportune moments.

The road to happiness is paved with golden opportunities. Each footstep taken on this journey is guaranteed a return of multimillions. The actions performed along the way become the pen to draw the lines of fortune. There is a greater share of happiness when individuals walk the path together, and through collective actions, draw the lines of fortune on the living landscape of the world.

ℋONESTY

Honesty means there are no contradictions or discrepancies in thoughts, words, or actions.

To be honest to one's real self and to the purpose of a task earns trust and inspires faith in others.

Honesty is never to misuse that which is given in trust.

Honesty is a clear conscience "before my self and before my fellow human beings." Honesty is the awareness of what is right and appropriate in one's role, one's behavior, and one's relationships. With honesty, there is no hypocrisy or artificiality which create confusion and mistrust in the minds and lives of others. Honesty makes for a life of integrity because the inner and outer selves are a mirror image.

Honesty is to speak that which is thought and to do that which is spoken. There are no contradictions or discrepancies in thoughts, words, or actions. Such integration provides clarity and example to others. To have one form internally and another form externally creates barriers and can cause damage, since one would neither be able to come close to anyone else, nor would others want to be close. Some think, "I am honest, but no one understands me." That is not honest. Honesty is as distinct as a flawless diamond which can never remain hidden. The worth is visible in one's actions.

Clouding Issues

Inner honesty needs to be examined to provide wisdom and support and ensure strength and stability. Positive firmness within creates an oasis of spiritual resources, giving confidence to be grounded in one's self-esteem. That is assertiveness. If internally there is attachment to a person, object, or idea, that attachment poses an obstacle to reality and objectivity, and action cannot be taken in the interest of the whole. The internal state should not be influenced by the negativity of one's nature, feelings, or personality traits. Selfish motives, hidden agendas, and negative feelings and habits are stains on the mirror of life. Honesty acts as the stain remover.

For self-growth, there should be cleanliness in one's efforts and truth in one's heart. Cleanliness means exploring and changing consciousness and activity which blemish the self and raise doubts in others. There should be honesty of the heart and also honesty of the head; otherwise, there will be self-deception or a tendency to deceive others by clouding issues with excuses or long-winded explanations. When the mirror of the self is clean, feelings, nature, motives, and objectives are clearly visible, and the individual reflects trustworthiness. There is the saying, "The boat of truth may rock, but it will never sink." Even with honesty, the boat sometimes rocks, but trustworthiness guarantees the boat will not sink. The courage of truth makes one worthy of trust.

To be trusted and to trust provide the foundation and cohesion necessary for untarnished relationships. It is also necessary to share with honesty the feelings and motives of one another. When there is honesty and cleanliness, there is also closeness. Without these principles, neither individuals nor societies can be functional.

Application and Experimentation

Personal and collective application of such ethics and principles involves experimenting to see what works best, to see what is meaningful and useful. Such is a continuous process of application and learning. Progress comes through experimenting with honesty and implementing it as completely and sincerely as possible at any given moment. When there is the experience of success, commitment to honesty and integrity is strengthened. To carry out a task out of force, compulsion, or with a careless or selfish attitude does not reflect pure motives. To be honest with one's real self and true to the purpose of a task earns trust and inspires faith in others. For progress to be sustained requires purity of motive and consistency of effort.

An honest person is one who aspires to follow the highest codes of conduct, who is loyal to the benevolent and universal principles of life, and whose decisions are based clearly on what is right and wrong. Such an individual maintains standards which provide guidance and courage to understand and respect the subtle connections of the world in relation to his or her life. An honest person appreciates the interconnectedness of the natural world and does not misuse, abuse, or waste the wealth of resources provided for the well-being of humanity. An honest person does not take for granted his or her own resources such as mind, body, wealth, time, talents, or knowledge.

Honesty means never to misuse that which is given in trust. There would always be the concern that resources be used in a worthwhile way - for the basic human, moral, and spiritual needs of all people. Well-used resources create well-being and are a means for those very resources to multiply. The individual who is deeply committed to development and progress keeps honesty as a constant principle in building a world of peace and plenty, a world of less expenditure and greater splendor.

$\mathscr{H}$UMILITY

*A person who embodies humility
will make the effort to listen to
and accept others.*

*The greater the acceptance of others,
the more that person will be held
in high esteem, and the more that person
will be listened to.*

*One word spoken in humility has the
significance of a thousand words.*

Humility is found in a vast ocean of still waters which run very deep. At the bottom lies self-esteem. At first, going within the ocean is like journeying into an unknown area of immense darkness. But, just as exploration can lead to buried treasures, one searching his or her inner world can find jewels buried in the depths. And the jewel buried deepest – which shines the brightest and gives the most light – is humility. At the darkest moments, its rays penetrate. It removes fear and insecurity and opens up the self to universal truths.

Trusteeship

Humility is to accept natural principles which cannot be controlled. Everything we have – from the bodies we were born into to our most prized possessions – is inherited. It therefore becomes a moral imperative to use those assets in a worthwhile and benevolent way. The consciousness of being a trustee of such unlimited and timeless resources touches the core of the human soul and awakens it to the realization that, just as at the time of birth such resources were inherited, at the time of death they will be left behind. In death, all that will accompany the individual will be the impressions of how those resources were used, combined with the wisdom of being and living as a trustee.

The consciousness of trusteeship heightens one's self-esteem and enhances the many different relationships encountered throughout life. It draws one into a mode of silent reflection, inviting one to take time out and look at life from a different perspective. It is as if the recognition of trusteeship causes the individual to seek renewal of the relationships to the self and to the world.

Removing 'I' and 'Mine'

Humility is to let go and let be. The stone of conflict lies in the consciousness of 'I' and 'mine' and in possessiveness - over a role, an activity, an object, a person, even the physical body. Paradoxically, such a consciousness makes one lose that which he or she wants to hold onto - most significantly, the universal values which give worth and meaning to life. Humility eliminates possessiveness and narrow vision which create physical, intellectual, and emotional boundaries. Such limitations destroy self-esteem and build walls of arrogance and pride, which distance others. Humility gently works on the crevices to allow for breakthroughs.

When one has the virtue of humility, everyone 'bows down,' since everyone bows to those who themselves bow first. Thus, the sign of greatness is humility. Humility enables the individual to become dependable, flexible, and adaptable. To the extent one becomes humble is the degree to which one becomes great in everyone's heart. A person who embodies humility will make the effort to listen to and accept others. The greater the acceptance of others, the more that person will be held in high esteem, and the more that person will be listened to. Humility automatically makes one worthy of praise.

A Call to Serve

Success in service comes from humility. The greater the humility, the greater the achievement. There cannot be world benefit without humility. Service is best done when 1) one considers the self a trustee or an instrument, and 2) one takes the first step toward accepting another who is different.

A humble person is able to function in all environments, no matter how unfamiliar or negative. There would be humility in attitude, outlook, words, and in connections and relationships. The humble person would not say, "It wasn't in my attitude, but the words just emerged." No, whatever the attitude, the outlook would be accordingly; whatever the outlook, the words would reflect that; and the three combined would assure quality interactions. The mere presence of a humble person creates an inviting, cordial, and comfortable environment. His or her words are essenceful and powerful and spoken with good manners. A humble person can defuse someone's anger with just a few words. One word spoken in humility has the significance of a thousand words.

On the high tides of human interactions, humility is the lighthouse which provides signals of what to expect in the distance. To adhere to these signals, the screen of the mind and intellect must be clean. Humility gives the power to perceive situations, to discern causes of obstacles and difficulties, and to remain silent. When one does express an opinion, it is with an open mind and with recognition of specialties, strengths, and sensitivities of the self and others.

Humility as well as the concept of trusteeship embrace our relationship with nature and oblige us not to tamper with natural laws. Nature is as life-giving as an umbilical cord. To arrogantly exploit and damage the natural habitat is to put the entire human family at peril. Humility is to inculcate natural principles in personal behavior, relationships, and other areas of human development. Without humility, we can neither build civil societies nor serve the world benevolently.

𝓛OVE

In a better world, the
natural law is love; and in a
better person, the natural
nature is
loving.

*Love is the principle which creates
and sustains human relations with
dignity and depth.*

*Spiritual love takes one into silence,
and that silence has the power to unite,
guide, and free people.*

*Love is the bedrock for the belief in
equality of spirit and personhood.*

*When love is combined with faith,
that creates a strong foundation for
initiative and action.*

*Love is the catalyst for change,
development, and achievement.*

Love is not simply a desire, a passion, an intense feeling for one person or object, but a consciousness which is simultaneously selfless and self-fulfilling. Love can be for one's country, for a cherished aim, for truth, for justice, for ethics, for people, for nature, for service, and for God. Love flows from truth, that is, wisdom. Love based on wisdom is real love, not blind love; and to discover the secrets of love is to watch the secrets of life unfold.

Basis of True Love

The basis of real love between people is spiritual. To see another as a spiritual being, a soul, is to see the spiritual reality of the other. To be conscious of that reality is to have spiritual love: each person, complete within, independent yet totally interconnected, recognizes that state in the other. As a result, there is constant and natural love. True love is when the soul has love for the soul. Love for the soul is eternal; the soul never dies. Such love is righteous, and it brings joy. Attachment to that which is perishable is unrighteous, and it brings sorrow.

When spiritual love prevails, neither internal nor external animosity, hatred, anger, or jealousy are possible. Negative feelings are transformed into positive feelings with the coolness of love. In spiritual love there is harmony, since love removes controlling or codependent tendencies and ensures kindness, caring, and amicable understanding.

Coolness of Love

Spiritual love means not dwelling on the weaknesses of others. Instead, there is concern for removing one's own defects. The method to do that is to "check one's own pulse" regularly to monitor how much one has adopted the natural habit of giving happiness, not sorrow, to others. However, true love from the heart also means one cannot bear to see weaknesses in another for whom there is love. There is the pure desire to correct what is inaccurate. Such correction would be carried out, on one hand, with the feeling of love, and on the other hand, with the power of words. There would be balance between the two. When there is too much force in the words or too much love, the result is not successful. If words are too sharp, another may be insulted or put off by bossiness. When one has the right balance of love and power in words, that gives others an experience of compassion, mercy, and benefit. No matter how powerful or bitter the message, it will touch the heart of the other and will be experienced as truth.

Human beings have become caught up in a pattern of behavior which has distorted the value of love and the ability to trust one another with feelings and intentions. One minute there is love; the next minute that love is broken, resulting in intense sorrow and pain. It is as if the human intellect has lost connection with the One eternal source of love and has taken support from temporary sources. As a result, instead of having one strength and one support from an unconditional source, human souls remain thirsty for true love, even one drop. Without that love, they continue to wander around in distress, searching . . . .

The Eternal Flame

The world remembers God as the ultimate source of love, the Ocean of Love, the Eternal Flame. God gives - unconditionally - love that is imperishable, universal, and unique. Imperishable in that the love is unlimited, constantly radiating, and totally available. Universal in that the love holds no boundaries or preferences; loving vibrations emanate to all souls of all cultures, races, and creeds. Unique in that the fire of God's love cleans the heart and soul. Those who tap into such love re-establish the bond of an eternal relationship. Those who experience the spiritual love of God - who 'merge with the Eternal Flame of Truth' - are disconnected from falsehood. Such souls have learned the first lesson of universal brotherhood: that all souls have love for one another because they are children of the same Parent. That is called spiritual love.

When the fire of spiritual love has been ignited, individuals begin exercising the will power to set themselves free from bondages of short-lived gratification. Time is invested and effort is made to build an internal stage in which love is revealed on the face and in every activity. With the enlightenment of spiritual love, individuals are less disturbed by adverse circumstances. They view dark clouds and storms as opportunities to exercise their internal strength and resources. If others do not give them love, that does not extinguish their flame. They overcome thoughts which may direct them to step away from a particular person, place, or task. Instead, there is the faith that with effort, they will make a significant and beneficial difference. The more effort is made to love, the more love is received. The spark of effort is love, and true love for effort means to remove whatever weaknesses stand in the way of love.

An entire world can be transformed through loving vision, loving attitude, and loving actions. To create a better world - a world of truth - spiritual love is primary. In a better world, the natural law is love; and in a better person, the natural nature is loving.

PEACE

In its purest form,
peace is inner silence filled with
the power of truth.

Peace is the prominent characteristic of
what we call 'a civilized society,'
and the character of a society can be seen
through the collective consciousness
of its members.

The challenge to peace normally presents itself in the question, "Are human beings by nature violent or nonviolent?" If the answer is violent, then the concept of peace becomes nonexistent. Peace has become so illusive that people have begun to question its existence. Peace of mind has become a popular cliché, but what does that mean?

What Is Peace?

Peace is energy, a qualitative energy which emanates constantly from the One imperishable source. It is a pure force that penetrates the shell of chaos, and by its very nature automatically puts things and people into balanced order. The self is a reservoir of vital resources, one of which is peace. To recognize the original quality of the human soul as peace is to stop searching outside for peace. Through connection with the One eternal and unlimited source of peace, our own reservoirs overflow with silent strength. In its purest form, peace is inner silence filled with the power of truth.

Peace consists of pure thoughts, pure feelings, and pure wishes. When the energy of thought, word, and action is balanced, stable, and nonviolent, the individual is at peace with the self, in relationships, and with the world. To exercise the power of peace embraces the fundamental principle of spirituality: look inward in order to look outward with courage, purpose, and meaning. The first step in that process takes careful examination of one's thoughts, feelings, and motives. By opening the window of the inner self, individuals are able to clarify and pinpoint attitudes and behavior patterns which are destructive, causing chaos and peacelessness.

Peacelessness Begins

People say in one breath that they want peace of mind, and in the next breath they say hurtful things. Wasteful gossip spreads peacelessness, as does anger. Peacelessness initially begins with a few angry, forceful thoughts which are then expressed in words and in some instances escalate into uncontrolled proportions of violence.

People say they want peace in the world, but what kind of peace do they desire? People ask for peace, but whose responsibility is that? Can anyone who remains peaceless be an instrument for peace? Authenticity of action depends on authenticity of person. Today, policymakers are dedicated to making, building, and keeping peace. A tremendous amount of human resources and research is invested in establishing world peace. Even prizes are given to people for their work toward peace. Emphasis is placed on the value of peace precisely because of the great peacelessness that exists and which has infiltrated our lives far deeper than we care to admit.

In its most common form, peacelessness can be felt as stress and pressure due to family, work, social, and other obligations. In its more serious condition, peacelessness is manifested in breakdowns, addictions, abuse, crime, emotional imbalances, and psychosomatic ailments. While medical science has helped relieve symptoms of stress, and psychology has contributed toward understanding the psyche, there continues a genuine search for a functional and empowering spirituality which can produce within the individual a calm and relaxed state of mind. The inner qualities and thought power of human beings are fast being recognized as tools to deal with the world and its growing demands. Health is being examined from a holistic perspective, partnering both physical and spiritual energies in the process of healing. Even when physical health is maintained, spiritual resources are being tapped to enhance coping skills and interpersonal relations.

Promise of Peace

The promise of peace gives hope, but like a piece of quicksilver, it sometimes seems slippery and evasive. We are at a crossroads of human civilization. On one hand, things are rapidly disintegrating. That is made bitterly apparent by wars, civil strife, riots, ethnic cleansing, and so on. However, on the other hand, an almost invisible integration involving alternatives and possibilities is putting the pieces together. Bringing peace back into the social, economic, political, and other fibers of society would require looking at peace from two levels: the external and the internal. Peace education, conflict resolution, and all peace initiatives must take seriously the critical connection between individual and world peace. Programs and projects must include an emphasis on individual peace, offering proactive and practical means to peace, beginning with the first step of knowing the inner self.

Peace is the foundation, the major building block upon which a healthy, functional society stands. Peace is the prominent characteristic of what we call "a civilized society," and the character of a society can be seen through the collective consciousness of its members. A civilization can be heaven or hell depending on the consciousness of its members. Consciousness creates culture – its norms, values, and systems – and consciousness can transform culture.

Ultimately, when all minds are focused and stabilized on the One imperishable source of peace and synchronized throughout the world, the reverberation of peace emitted from the silence will echo, "WORLD PEACE IS DECLARED!"

RESPECT

To know one's own worth and to honor
the worth of others is the true way
to earn respect.

Respect is an acknowledgment of the
inherent worth and innate rights of the
individual and the collective.

These must be recognized as the central
focus to draw from people a commitment
to a higher purpose in life.

Respect begins within the individual. The original state of respect is based on awareness of the self as a unique entity, a life force within, a spiritual being, a soul. The elevated consciousness of knowing "who I am" arises from an authentic place of pure worth. With such insight, there is faith in the self and wholeness and completeness within. With self-realization, one experiences true self-respect.

Source of Conflict

Conflict is initiated when the awareness of one's original nature and the original nature of the other is lacking. As a result, external negative influences rule supreme over respect. To be stabilized in the elevated stage of the self ensures genuine respect for and from others, since one acts in the consciousness that every human being has innate worth which is pure and virtuous. Such a mindset guarantees ultimate victory, since interaction on that basis assures that the inherent goodness of the self and the other emerges.

The beginning of all weakness is the absence of one word: self. When the word self is removed from self-respect, the void is filled by a variety of desires or expectations, each specifically designed to claim regard or respect from others. The individual, having become dependent on external forces rather than internal powers, then measures respect by physical and material factors, such as caste, color, race, religion, sex, nationality, status, and popularity. The more respect is measured on the basis of something external, the greater the desire for recognition from others. The greater the desire, the more one falls victim and loses respect - for the self and from others. If individuals renounced the desire of receiving regard and stabilized themselves in the elevated stage of self-respect, then regard would follow like a shadow.

To develop the value of respect within the self and to give it practical expression in daily life is the challenge. Obstacles are encountered to test the strength of respect, and these are often felt at the most vulnerable times. Self-confidence is needed to deal with circumstances in an optimistic, hopeful, and self-assured manner. In situations when all supports seem to have vanished, what remains loyal is the extent to which one has been able to become self-reliant internally.

Respectful Environment

The power of discernment establishes a respectful environment in which attention is paid to the quality of intentions, attitude, behavior, thoughts, words, and actions. To the extent that there is the power of humility in respecting the self - and the discernment and wisdom that affords in being just and fair to others – there will be success in the form of valuing individuality, appreciating diversity, and taking the complete task into consideration. The balance of humility and self-respect results in selfless service, an honorable act, devoid of debilitating attitudes such as arrogance and narrow-mindedness. Arrogance damages or destroys the uniqueness of others and violates their fundamental rights. Such a temperament hurts the violator as well. For example, the tendencies to impress, dominate, or limit the freedom of others are each done with the aim of asserting the self but at the expense of inner worth, dignity, and peace of mind. Original respect becomes subservient to an artificial one.

Thus, attempting to win respect without remaining conscious of one's original worth and honor becomes the very method to lose respect. To know one's own worth and to honor the worth of others is the true way to earn respect. Since such a principle originates in that pristine place of pure worth, others instinctively sense authenticity and sincerity. In the vision and attitude of equality, there is shared spirituality. Sharing creates a sense of belonging, a feeling of family.

That sense of honor and worth can extend to nature's family. To show disrespect and to work against the laws of nature is to cause ecological imbalances and natural calamities. When respect and reverence are extended to the eternal energy of matter, the elements will serve humanity with accuracy and abundance.

Respect is an acknowledgment of the inherent worth and innate rights of the individual and the collective. These must be recognized as the central focus to draw from people a commitment to a higher purpose in life. International respect and recognition for intellectual rights and originality of ideas must be observed without discrimination. The eminence of life is present in everyone, and every human being has a right to the joy of living with respect and dignity.

$\mathscr{R}$ESPONSIBILITY

*A responsible person fulfills
the assigned duty by staying true
to the aim.*

*Duties are carried out with integrity and
a sense of purpose.*

Circumstances, necessity, and choice place people in particular situations and roles. Moral responsibility is to accept what is required, to honor the role which has been entrusted, and to perform conscientiously and to the best of one's ability. The actor has been given the part. He or she should be mindful of that and not wish to be somewhere or someone else. Duties should be carried out with integrity and a sense of purpose.

Acting Responsibly

Personal responsibility in life comes from many expected and unexpected sources and involves partnership and participation, commitment and cooperation. Social and global responsibility requires all the above as well as justice, humaneness, and respect for the rights of all human beings. Particular attention is paid to ensure that benefit is for all without discrimination.

Some interpret responsibility as a burden and fail to see it as personally relevant. It becomes convenient to project it as someone else's problem. These people deny their responsibility, yet when it comes to rights, they are the first in line!

A responsible person perseveres, not stubbornly with a blind focus, but with the motivation of fulfilling the assigned duty by staying true to the aim. When there is the consciousness of being an instrument or a facilitator, a person stays neutral and flexible in his or her role. One remains detached yet has a clear understanding of what needs to be done. When the role is played accurately, there is efficiency and effectiveness which result in satisfaction and contentment at having made a significant contribution.

Responsibility often calls upon humility to help overcome obstacles created by ego. For instance, one acting responsibly does not take over or control the outcome. One acting responsibly also has the maturity to know when a responsibility should be handed to another. A major barrier is becoming too attached to the responsibility. Being over-conscientious leads to worry, doubt, and fear, which can have a crippling effect on decision-making and result in devastating consequences.

Collaboration Is Essential

Responsible individuals work in collaboration. That is true for all tasks and especially important in areas which affect the lives of others. Responsible individuals operate on two premises: 1) that all participants have something worthwhile to offer, and 2) that the situation requires a cooperative rather than a competitive environment. Responsible people do not fall into the traps of inferiority or superiority; they recognize that the optimum outcome cannot depend on one person, one group, or one nation alone.

Responsibility is managing time and resources to bring maximum benefit while accommodating necessary change. Decisions in the consciousness of being responsible for social or global welfare encourage actions which are performed in a selfless way. In taking responsibility for others' rights, a budget of all assets - mental, physical, and spiritual - needs to be devised. That includes taking into account accumulated and available resources and their efficient and equitable use. Inattention, carelessness, corruption, greed, or lack of judgment result not only in some people or areas receiving nothing, some not enough, and others too much, but also in the unnecessary loss of human lives and natural resources.

Accountability

Whether the act is for world or for individual improvement, when that role and responsibility are accepted, there needs to be an internal support system which ensures that essential qualities are assimilated and put into practical activity. Such is necessary for everyone and especially so for parents, educators, religious leaders, political leaders, and celebrities, as well as trendsetters from various disciplines, since they are all role models of behavior. They have significant roles because they help shape norms which have enormous influence on weaving the fabric of society. One principle of learning is observing the behavior and real-life experience of those we admire and respect. Therefore, it is incumbent upon role models to accept and honor the responsibility of being "examples." The bigger the part, the greater the concern should be for the message being imparted and its impact on the lives of others.

It has been said that with rights go responsibilities, and within that concept the law of action becomes operable. Each human being is like a star consisting of his or her own small world. Each star has to perceive its own world and look for the balance of rights and responsibilities. Life is the field of action. On that field, each one's part should be enacted with responsibility and accountability. Those who wear the crown of responsibility embedded with the jewels of rights become the stars with a positive influence on the world!

$\mathscr{S}$IMPLICITY

*Simplicity calls on instinct, intuition,
and insight to create essenceful thoughts
and empathetic feelings.*

*Simplicity is the conscience which calls
upon people to rethink their values.*

Simplicity grows from sacred roots, embodying a wealth of spiritual virtues and values made apparent by attitude, words, activities, and lifestyle. Simplicity is beautiful, and like the moon, it radiates coolness in contrast to the effulgence of the sun. Simplicity is natural. It may appear common and without appeal to those whose vision has become habituated by superficiality. However, to those with an artist's refined insight, a glimpse of simplicity is enough to recognize the masterpiece.

Simple Living, High Thinking

Simplicity combines sweetness and wisdom. It is plainness of mind and intellect. Those embodying simplicity are free from strenuous thinking and complicated, extraneous thoughts. The intellect is sharp and alert. Simplicity calls on instinct, intuition, and insight to create essenceful thoughts and empathetic feelings. There is egolessness in simplicity, as if one embodying that virtue has renounced possessiveness and is free from material desires which distract the intellect, causing it to wander into wasteful territory. Being without desire does not mean one goes without. On the contrary, one has everything, including inner fulfillment. That is apparent on the face - innocent of disturbance, weakness, and anger - and in the behavior - uniquely elegant and royal, yet naive. Simplicity is being the innocent child and the wise master. It teaches simple living and high thinking.

People living simply normally enjoy a close relationship with nature. Their ethic is derived from perennial traditions operating according to the laws of nature. They rise at dawn and retire at dusk. They tell the time of day by the position of the sun and determine the dates of sacred days by the position of the moon. Herbs become their natural cures, the backyard their farmers' market, and the moon and stars their light bulbs. The natural world is their classroom. This does not mean that all should adopt such a lifestyle. However, there are lessons to be learned in nature. When the ethic of simplicity is followed, there is hardly any waste. All resources, time, thoughts, ideas, knowledge, money, and raw materials are valued as investments.

From simplicity grows generosity. Generosity is sharing hard-earned income with liberality of spirit. Sharing one's own resources in a congenial and caring manner is to bring back to human activity the meaning of family. Simplicity is more than giving money and material possessions. It is giving of the self that which is priceless - patience, friendship, and encouragement. In the spirit of putting others first, those embracing simplicity donate their time freely to others. That is done with kindness, openness, and pure intentions and without expectations and conditions. As a result, such individuals reap the abundant fruits sown from the seeds of generous actions.

Beauty Is Truth

Simplicity is truth. The beauty of truth is so simple, it works like alchemy. No matter how many disguises may come in front of it, the light of truth cannot remain hidden; it will reach out to the masses in a language so simple yet with a message so profound. The messengers of truth have always embodied ordinary forms, led simple lives, and adopted simple mediums of imparting their messages. They lived and spoke the truth, bringing beauty to the lives of others. In their simplicity and splendor, they can be compared to the jeweller. While remaining true to the integrity of his profession, the jeweller makes every single jewel flawless and precious, but he himself remains simple.

Today beauty is defined by the fashion and beauty industries, amplified by the rich and famous, and embraced by the masses. Beauty, however, is not only skin deep, as the saying goes. Beauty in its simplest form is about removing the arrogance of expensive clothing and extravagant living. Beauty goes beyond rich and poor. It is appreciating the small things in life, sometimes not visible or apparent to the rest of the world. Simplicity is appreciating inner beauty and recognizing the value of all actors, even the poorest and worst off. It is considering all tasks, including the most menial, to have worth and dignity.

Ethic of Simplicity

The ethic of simplicity is the precursor to sustainable development. Simplicity teaches economy. It teaches investment by example to those clear and honest about their needs and who live accordingly. Simplicity is the conscience which calls upon people to rethink their values. Simplicity asks whether we are being induced to purchase unnecessary products. Psychological enticements create artificial needs. Desires stimulated by wanting unnecessary things result in value clashes complicated by greed, fear, peer pressure, and a false sense of identity. Once fulfillment of basic necessities allows for a comfortable lifestyle, extremes and excesses invite overindulgence and waste. While that approach can be defended as a means to build certain economies, it should not be used at the expense of pushing other economies into dire poverty. It should not be that imposed sacrifice of some brings great affluence to others. That is not a principle but an injustice!

Simplicity helps decrease the gap between "the haves" and "the have nots" by demonstrating the logic of true economics: to earn, save, invest, and share the sacrifices and the prosperity so that there can be a better quality of life for all people regardless of where they were born.

TOLERANCE

*Through understanding and
open-mindedness, a tolerant person
attracts someone different,
and by genuinely accepting and
accommodating that person demonstrates
tolerance in practical form.*

The world – our extended family of people – can be depicted as a large tree with many limbs, branches, and shoots. Each nation – represented by a limb – is a brother or a sister having families of their own. Those families – represented by branches – are the various provinces and communities made up of all religions and ethnic groups. When the roots of history are seen by placement of family members on such a genealogical tree, that perspective shows complementarity among all people and demonstrates that coexistence is possible. Since the tree takes sustenance from common, original roots which grew from one seed, the human family tree can be no different. Coexistence stems from the very seed from which life sprang! And tolerance, which also develops from that one seed, not only has roots which run deep and which sustain, but also expresses itself in other diverse ways, including enriching the soil and providing showers of acceptance and support.

Coexistence

The aim of tolerance is peaceful coexistence. While tolerance recognizes individuality and diversity, it removes divisive masks and defuses tension created by ignorance. It provides opportunity to discover and remove stereotypes and stigmas associated with people perceived to be different because of nationality, religion, or heritage. Just as a gardener recognizes characteristics of each variety of seed and prepares the grounds accordingly, a tolerant person takes into consideration the uniqueness of all people. Through understanding and open-mindedness, a tolerant person attracts someone different; and by genuinely accepting and accommodating that person, demonstrates tolerance in practical form. As a result, relationships blossom.

The seed of tolerance, love, is sown with compassion and care. The more one becomes loving and shares that love, the greater the power in that love. When there is lack of love, there is lack of tolerance. For instance, the example of mother and child: when an obstacle comes to a child, because the mother has love for that child, she is prepared to and has the power to tolerate anything. At that time, she does not worry about her own well-being but uses love to confront all circumstances. Love makes anything easier to tolerate.

Family is the first classroom to learn tolerance, as there is always some adjustment to be made to accommodate others. School is the second classroom. However, tests of tolerance are taken each and every day of one's life. Those who pass most often have the consciousness of appreciating the good in people and in situations. Those receiving lower marks usually have shades or degrees of disapproval. And those who pass with honor use the power of tolerance as a shield of protection so that internal serenity remains untouched.

Discrimination in Decision-Making

Tolerance is inner strength which enables the individual to face and transform misunderstandings and difficulties. The method for that is first to use discrimination in decision-making. By delving into the conscience, one can determine what is right or wrong; what will bring benefit or loss; and what will bring short- or long-term attainment. Insightful decisions result. The power of decision-making eliminates upheaval in the mind and intellect as well as between emotion and reason. There is neither conflict within the self nor with others, since tolerance cultivates the ability to cool the strong and heated feelings of others. Even if insults were thrown, there would not be the slightest sign of wilting visible on the face. Knowledge and insight automatically raise the protective shield of tolerance so that the individual stays full and content and not threatened by people or circumstance. A tolerant person is like a tree with an abundance of fruits. Even when pelted with sticks and stones, the tree gives its fruit in return.

In official and professional settings, the fruit of one's intentions and actions can be damaged if – when interacting with colleagues – the protective canopy of tolerance does not shade the tree. Those who have the power to tolerate do not allow negative external vibrations to cloud their minds and cause doubt and discontentment. There is inner contentment. They are able to see things as they are rather than what they appear to be and to take necessary action.

Ability to Accommodate

Certain circumstances often demand tolerance. Extremities of seasons and varying levels of bodily pain are cases in point. The artisans of science and technology have been invaluable in assisting human beings to accommodate extreme heat and cold, and advanced medical treatment has done wonders in helping individuals tolerate pain. Yet, such benefits do not mean that discomfort is eliminated completely. At some level for all, and for some more so than others, tolerance becomes an indispensable power to cope.

Tolerance develops the ability to accommodate the problems of everyday living. The hundreds of people who rush to the train station after a hard day's work may be tired and weary. Their accommodation skills are tested when the announcement is heard: "All trains have been cancelled due to technical difficulties with the lines. Passengers are requested to use alternative routes." To tolerate life's inconveniences is to let go, be light, make others light, and move on. Mountains are made into molehills, and molehills are made into mustard seeds!

$\mathscr{U}$NITY

*Unity is harmony within and among
individuals in the group.*

*Unity is sustained by concentrating
energy and focusing thought, by accepting
and appreciating the value of the rich
array of participants and the unique
contribution each can make,
and by remaining loyal not only to one
another but also to the task.*

Unity is built from a shared vision, a cherished hope, an altruistic aim, or a cause for the common good. Unity gives sustenance, strength, and courage to make the impossible possible. Combining with determination and commitment, unity makes the biggest task seem easy.

The stability of unity comes from the spirit of equality and oneness, the noble values embodied in core universal principles. The greatness of unity is that everyone is respected. Unity creates the experience of cooperation, increases zeal and enthusiasm for the task, and makes the atmosphere powerful and enabling.

In Harmony

A gathering does not have unity until there is harmony within and among the individuals in the group. Just as the musician needs to practice playing the instrument alone before joining the symphony orchestra, the individual needs solitude to be in touch with his or her capacity, potential, and specialty before joining the gathering. For individual effectiveness, there needs to be clarity and cleanliness of motives and intentions. Looking inward helps harmonize thoughts, words, and actions; the individual can then adapt as necessary. Such personal integration keeps the individual "in tune."

The orchestra creates a consonance of sounds by combining the distinct rhythmic patterns of each of its instruments. In the same way, the gathering becomes sweetly harmonious when each individual adopts the power to accommodate the capacities and specialties of the others; modulates those with the self; and then combines with the orchestra. Unity is sustained by concentrating energy and focusing thought, by accepting and appreciating the value of the rich array of participants and the unique contribution each can make, and by remaining loyal not only to one another but also to the task. Such positive focus builds to a crescendo as oneness in diversity is experienced; and because unity inspires stronger personal commitment and greater collective achievement, dance as well as music can be attained!

Causes of Disunity

One note of disrespect can cause unity to be broken. Interrupting others, giving unconstructive and prolonged criticism, keeping watch over some or control over others are all strident chords which strike harshly at connections and relationships. Ego and inferiority produce disharmonious sounds. Such discord can be easily heard or quite subtle and can range from dwelling on weaknesses of others and hunger for recognition to jealousy, insecurity, and doubt.

Sometimes, even in little matters, people quickly get upset, aggressive, angry, or violent; they then isolate themselves into subgroups, producing dissension and conflict. Retuning and fine tuning then become essential.

A basic human need is to feel a sense of belonging, to be part of the unified whole. People do not want to remain in isolation, oblivious to the world outside. It is also uniquely human to be curious about other people and cultures and to feel a deep sense of compassion over sufferings of and injustices done to others. It is, therefore, human instinct to want to be together and to form natural gatherings or structured meetings which provide a common platform to talk to each other. In such ways, people get to know, understand, or help each other. This holds true for individuals as well as for nations. Consciously or unconsciously, we choose to be and act together.

Today, our curiosity is satisfied with the help of TV and the media, bringing people and cultures from around the world into our very living rooms. If that is not enough for some, travel can provide the firsthand experience! Humanity can take pride in its virtue as well as its ingenuity. Yet, with all its good, humanity is equally guilty of vice. With brothers seen as "enemies," vital energy is being misdirected, and the home of unity keeps shaking. As a result, humanity has not been able to sustain unity against the common enemies of civil war, ethnic conflict, poverty, hunger, and violation of human rights.

Inner Focus

Creating unity in the world begins with a change in individual consciousness. Such requires the human intellect to move away from conflict and confusion and – for a period of time on an ongoing basis – to concentrate in positive directions. Such inner focus does not isolate the individual, but, in fact, does the opposite: it brings that person closer to others, and in that closeness, in that shared humanity, there is the collective strength to pioneer and sustain fundamental and constructive transformation.

APPENDIX 1

ABOUT THE BRAHMA KUMARIS

The Brahma Kumaris World Spiritual University (BKWSU) focuses on understanding the self, its inner resources and strengths, and developing attributes of leadership and the highest level of personal integrity. The University's activities are grounded in the belief that the world needs to invest more resources in educating its peoples with sound human, moral, and spiritual values. It is not enough to enshrine values and ethics in institutions, systems, and constitutions, for even the best arrangements are of little use if people who implement them have wrong values.

To help facilitate the growing need for deeper research into universal values, the Brahma Kumaris recently built the Academy for a Better World. Located on a 23-acre site just three miles from the BK headquarters in Mt. Abu, India, the Academy - also known as Gyan Sarovar, meaning Lake of Knowledge in Hindi - serves as an international education and training facility. Designed and constructed to maximize the latest technologies in the fields of solar- and wind-generated power, the Academy can accommodate 1,200 people. It offers two large auditoriums, 13 training units, a library, playgrounds, environment park, alternative energy development building, laboratory and research section, museum, and an art gallery.

The Academy for a Better World is a common ground where professionals – managers, scientists, lawyers, doctors, educators, members of the media, healthcare workers, artists, and all others – can come together to explore and reflect on values. They research how values can be practiced as individuals and how that experience can impact one's profession in building value-based societies. Course offerings not only include open dialogues but also 5- to 30-day workshops in subjects such as self-empowerment, self-management, positive thinking, meditation, and practical spirituality.

The BKWSU, a non-governmental organization in consultative status with the United Nations Economic and Social Council and UNICEF, is an international organization with more than 3,500 centers in 65 countries. Established in 1937, the BKWSU "family" today consists of people from all backgrounds and denominations, who study a body of knowledge known as Raja Yoga. The knowledge is a practical method to help individuals achieve a deeper understanding of life and interact with others in a beneficial and fulfilling way.

The main spiritual heads and executive officers of the BKWSU are women.

APPENDIX 2

STEPS TOWARD A BETTER WORLD

The Brahma Kumaris have organized a number of major international projects designed to give individuals the opportunity to take steps toward a better world.

Million Minutes of Peace was dedicated to the United Nations International Year of Peace, 1986. That appeal, which asked people to pledge time in meditation, positive thinking, or prayers for peace, reached 88 countries and collected 1,231,975,713 minutes of peace. The total was equal to some 2,344 years of peace!

Global Cooperation for a Better World (GCBW), a follow-up to Million Minutes of Peace, was launched from the United Nations in New York and the Houses of Parliament in London in 1988. As an international Peace Messenger Initiative, GCBW had the support of more than 400 companies worldwide and involved tens of thousands of people. Essentially, GCBW elicited from people, in words or pictures, responses to the question: "What is your vision of a better world?" In answering that question, people were asked to observe one "Golden Rule," and that was to couch their responses in positive terms only. By 1990, the visions, hopes, and aspirations of a sweeping cross-section of individuals from more than 120 countries had been collected.

As a way of reporting on GCBW, Visions of a Better World, a Peace Messenger publication, was published. Dedicated to the world by the peoples of the world, the book features some of the vast outpouring of color and creativity produced by the GCBW project.

From the seeds of zeal and enthusiasm which took root when Visions of a Better World began spreading its positive message around the world, there grew the idea for another international initiative called Sharing Our Values for a Better World (SVBW). Dedicated to the United Nations on its 50th Anniversary (UN50), the year-long SVBW project started September, 1994 and will continue through September-October 1995, culminating in a month-long celebration to honor the UN50, at which time values will receive worldwide focus.

In preparation for the SVBW program, the Brahma Kumaris (BKs) assigned to each month of the year one of the 12 core values discussed in this booklet. Throughout the year, teachers and students in BK Centers worldwide have been organizing and focusing activities around that value. Activities include dialogues, seminars, workshops, lectures, and community projects. The object is to focus on achieving a deeper understanding and the practical application of that value for the month in the context of the local environment.

The 12 Value Statements contained in this booklet are excerpted from Living Values: A Guidebook, which is being used as a resource to help facilitate the SVBW project. In addition to the Value Statements, Living Values: A Guidebook contains two other major sections: 1) Individual Perspective, explaining in a light tone some of the premises and concepts in the Value Statements and offering tools and methods to help sustain positive change, and 2) Workshops and Activities, a variety of facilitated group sessions designed to help participants identify ways to "live" their values – at home, at work, at school, in the community, and in the global neighborhood.

For further information on Living Values: A Guidebook, contact a local Brahma Kumaris Center.

BRAHMA KUMARIS
WORLD SPIRITUAL UNIVERSITY

APPENDIX 3

WORLD HEADQUARTERS

BRAHMA KUMARIS WORLD SPIRITUAL UNIVERSITY
PO BOX NO.2, MOUNT ABU, RAJASTHAN 307501, INDIA

INTERNATIONAL COORDINATING OFFICE
AND EUROPEAN REGIONAL OFFICE
Global Co-operation House, 65 Pound Lane, London NW10 2HH, UK
Tel: (+44) 181 459 1400 Fax: (+44) 181 451 6480

REGIONAL OFFICES
AFRICA
PO Box 12349, Maua Close, off Parklands Road,
Nairobi, Kenya
Tel: (+254) 2 743 572 Fax: (+254) 2 743 885

AUSTRALIA AND SOUTH EAST ASIA
78 Alt Street, Ashfield, Sydney NSW 2131 Australia
Tel: (+61) 2 716 7066 Fax: (+61) 2 716 7795

NORTH AND SOUTH AMERICAS
Global Harmony House, 46 S. Middle Neck Road,
Great Neck, NY 11021 USA
Tel: (+1) 516 773 0971 Fax: (+1) 516 773 0976

Your Local Contact is: